Allen Linn's Children's Bible Book

Creation and the Life of Jesus

Allen Linn

Illustrations by Emily Zieroth

Copyright © 2020 by Allen Linn
Minneapolis, Minnesota
www.pyramidpublishers.com

All rights reserved. No part of this publication may be reproduced, stored in a retrieval system, or transmitted, in any form or by any means, electronic, mechanical, photocopying, recording, or otherwise, without the prior written permission of the author.

Printed by Lightning Source
1246 Heil Quaker Blvd.
La Vergne, TN USA 37086
ISBN – 978-0-9982014-8-1

Cover Design by Van-garde Imagery, Inc.
Illustrations by Emily Zieroth
Interior by Van-garde Imagery, Inc.
Printed in the United States of America

Unless otherwise noted, Scripture quotations are from
The Holy Bible, New International Version™, NIV™,
Copyright © 1973, 1978, 1984, 2011 by Biblica, Inc.™
Used by permission of Zondervan

Dedication

This book is dedicated to a little girl named Iris who loved Jesus and went home to be with Him in heaven. She is now happily in the arms of Jesus and has been an inspiration even to grown-ups. Her message to you is not to wait until you are grown up to live for Jesus but do it now while you are little.

The Bible

The Bible is the story of God and mankind. It tells how God created the world and how men and women did a foolish thing and went away from God. But because God loved us so much, He came after us to save us from the great danger we were in.

Who Wrote the Bible?

God caused men to write the words of the Bible that He gave them in order to tell the story He wanted told. The first writer of the Bible was Moses. God wanted mankind to know that even though they had done something so very wrong that He still loved them very much and wanted them to come back into His family.

Who Is God?

At first there was only God. He always existed. Because He is so great there are many things about God that are very hard to understand even for very smart grown-ups. There are not enough books to tell all there is to know about God, but here are seven things that can help you understand Him.

1. One of these things is that God always existed; He never had a beginning. He was always alive. That's hard for even grown-ups to understand; but that's what the Bible says, and what the Bible says is the truth.
2. God is so powerful that He can do anything He wants to do. There is nothing He cannot do.
3. God can be everywhere at the same time.
4. God knows everything. There is nothing He does not know. He even knows what we are thinking.
5. God can make anything out of nothing.
6. God is very loving and kind and forgives us our sins even though we don't deserve it.
7. He is three Persons in One God. There is only one God, but in this one God there are three Persons. They are the Father, the Son, and the Holy Spirit. They always do everything together.

God Created the World

God decided to make the world with all its plants and animals. He created men and woman so He could love them and they could love Him. He also created the angels.

God tells us how this happened in the first three chapters of Genesis, the first book of the Bible.

"In the beginning God made the heavens and the earth." God the Father wanted heaven and earth to be made so God the Son went out and made the heavens and the earth. "The beginning" is when God made time. God always existed but time had a beginning. When time began is when God made the heavens and the earth. "The heavens" at first were empty space; no stars or planets were made yet. And the earth was not finished. It was only a big rock mixed with some clay, mud, and dirt and covered by water. This was only the start of His home for mankind.

"God's plan was to make mankind, both men and women. He would make a special place just for them to show His love for them. He also made animals for us to love and care for and angels to help us and be our friends.

Let There Be Light

Then God the Holy Spirit hovered above the waters of the earth, getting everything ready for animal life and human life. God said let there be light, and there was light and it was glorious! God called the light "day" and He called the darkness "night." And the evening and the morning were the first day.

God next made the sky above the waters, and He moved the waters around to different places until dry land was seen. He called the dry ground "land" and called the waters "seas." God saw that it was good, and evening and morning were the second day.

Then God made the grass and flowers to make the earth beautiful. He made plants and vegetables and fruit trees with seeds in them that would grow more fruits and vegetables to feed the animals and mankind when He would make them. And evening and morning were the third day.

After that, God made the sun, moon, and stars to give light on the earth. The sun gave light on the earth during the day and the moon and stars gave light on the earth at night. And evening and morning were the fourth day.

Then God filled the waters with all kinds of living things from little tiny fish to huge whales and everything in between. He did the same in the sky: He filled it with birds of all kinds. God saw that it was good and told the living things in the waters and sky to have many babies. And evening and morning were the fifth day.

Then God filled the dry land with all kinds of animals, and He saw that it was good and told them to have many babies.

God Created Humans

Last of all God made mankind, both male and female. First He made the man, Adam. He took some dust and made something like clay and formed Adam's body and then very lovingly breathed into Adam and gave Him life. Then God made a lovely Garden and placed the man in the garden. It was called Eden and was watered by four rivers flowing through it. It was paradise. Then God took one of Adam's ribs and made a woman. Adam and Eve were special because they were made like God in some ways. They knew right from wrong and knew and loved God. God put them in charge of all the animals – to care for them and love them, and the animals loved Adam and Eve back.

God told them to have many babies and cover the whole world with people. God had already filled the earth with all kinds of vegetables and fruit trees from which other vegetables and trees would grow. He did this to provide never ending food for all mankind.

And God saw everything He had made and it was wonderful. Everything was just right. There was no pain and no hard work to do. There was no death, hunger, sickness, sorrow, disease, or loneliness. There was plenty of food to eat and perfect weather.

Satan

Before the creation of the world, God had created the angels. One of the most powerful angels was called Lucifer. He was very beautiful and bright and shining. He was even called the "son of the morning" and "the shining one." Instead of being thankful to God, he became very proud. One day he decided to take God's place and have everyone worship him instead of God, so God threw him out of heaven to earth, where he was known as Satan.

Satan knew God was too powerful for him to defeat in battle, so he decided to turn mankind away from God. When Satan saw how much God loved mankind and wanted them to love Him and obey Him, he realized the best way to hurt God was to make Adam and Eve disobey Him and put their trust in themselves instead of God.

To do that, Satan knew he would have to lie to Adam and Eve. Even today lies are Satan's best weapon, and the truth is his greatest enemy. His goal is to blind men and women from seeing God as He really is. The Lord Jesus said he was a murderer and a liar from the beginning. He could not tell the truth because there was no truth in him (John 8:44).

Two very special trees grew in the middle of the Garden of Eden. One was the Tree of Life, and the other was the Tree of the Knowledge of Good and Evil. God commanded Adam and Eve not to eat from the second tree. If they didn't eat of it, they would obey God and only know good. If they did eat of it, they would disobey God and know evil. Their choice was to go God's way and be happy or go their own way and bring sin into the world.

The Temptation Part One

Love is not love unless you have a choice not to love, so God gave them that choice with the Tree of the Knowledge of Good and Evil. He told them they could never eat fruit from this tree. If they obeyed God, good things would happen to them. If they disobeyed God, bad things would happen to them.

Satan knew he had to tempt them to eat from this tree because he knew that if they did, they would be under his control instead of God's control. Satan was very sneaky and took on the body of a snake to lie to them and turn them away from God.

In the beginning, serpents, or snakes as we call them today, were not scary and ugly and did not crawl on the ground like they do now. They were cute and loveable and stood upright and glided on their tails. Satan, the evil one, fools people even today because he talks so nice and friendly. He glided over to the woman and said: "I could not help but overhear, did God really tell you that you could not eat from all these trees? Did He really say that there was one special tree that you could not eat of? I find that hard to believe."

"It's true", Eve said, "God told us that we shouldn't eat from the tree of the knowledge of good and evil or we'll die. The serpent rolled his eyes. "I can't believe God told you that! He told you a lie because He was jealous of you. You will not surely die!

"Look", he lowered his voice and whispered, "God knows that when you eat of that tree, you will become like Him and you will not need to listen to God because you will be able to decide for yourself what is good and evil."

The Temptation Part Two

Now when she looked at the tree it seemed even more delightful. And the thought of becoming wise enough to make her own decisions without God made her want to eat the fruit even more. So she reached and took a piece of the forbidden fruit and ate. Then Adam came and saw what she did and she gave him some to eat.

When they ate of the forbidden fruit, their eyes were opened and they saw what they had done. They were ashamed of themselves for disobeying God. When they heard God in the Garden coming to visit them, which usually made them very happy and excited, they hid themselves.

God called out in a sad voice, "Where are you?"

Adam said, "I heard You in the garden and I was so ashamed that I hid myself."

God said, "Why were you ashamed? Did you eat of the tree that I commanded you not to eat of?"

Adam answered, "The woman you gave to be with me, she gave me of the fruit and I ate." Then God said to the woman, "What is this that you have done?" She answered, "The serpent deceived me and I ate".

Then the Lord said to the serpent, "Because you have done this, you will be punished. From now on you will crawl in the dirt and eat dust. I will send a Savior to mankind, and He will crush your head in utter defeat and you will cause Him pain and suffering but He will destroy you."

God Sends Adam and Eve Away

God told Adam and Eve that instead of living in the nice, comfortable garden, they would have to work hard to live. The ground would be cursed and be hard and rocky and full of weeds and thorns.

Their bodies would have aches and pains from hard work. Satan, the devil, became the ruler of the world and bad things started happening to people. Now there would be death, disease, and destruction – things like floods and hurricanes. There would be pain and sorrow.

God drove them out of the wonderful garden where they used to fellowship with God. Now they were separated from Him, the worst thing possible. And God set a mighty angel to keep them out of the garden and the Tree of Life. But He promised to send them a Savior, the Lord Jesus Christ, who would come in the future to save mankind and restore what Satan, the evil one, had ruined.

They were sad to leave the garden and enter a world of pain and heartbreak, but they had the happy thought of the Savior who would come and save all mankind from the curse of the fallen world. Jesus one day would save the world from sin and separation from God. He would bring men and women and boys and girls back into the Kingdom of God and take them into heaven when they died.

Abraham

One day God called a man named Abraham and told him to leave his country and go to a place that God would show him. He was told that one of his descendants would be the Savior who would defeat the devil, and the whole world would be blessed because of Him.

The land God led him to would later become the land of Israel. Israel was to be a very special land, whose people God would use to write the Bible. Many great heroes would come from there, including the mighty King David. And from this people and King David, Jesus the Savior would come.

There were great men called prophets who came from Israel after Abraham. These were special men that God used to write much of the Old Testament of the Bible. Many of them told of the coming Savior, God's own Son, who would become a human and rescue us from the power of the devil. And He would give new life from heaven to those who would love Him and believe in Him.

The Coming of Jesus Part One

When God saw that it was the right time to send His Son Jesus into the world, He visited a young girl named Mary in a town called Nazareth. She was a descendant of King David.

Mary was a good person who loved the Lord God and tried with all her heart to serve Him. She was soon to marry a carpenter named Joseph, who was a good man who also loved the Lord.

God sent the angel Gabriel with a wonderful and amazing message for her. "Greetings, God is with you and has highly favored you," he said.

Mary wondered what the angel meant. Then Gabriel said, "Do not be afraid for God has chosen you for something very special. Soon God is going to help you have a baby, a Son, and you are to name Him Jesus. He will be very great and will be the Son of the Most High God. God will give Him the throne of His ancestor David, and He will utterly defeat Satan and win the world back from him. And He will rule forever and ever. His kingdom shall never end.

But Mary said, "Sir I don't understand how this could happen. I'm not even married."

The angel answered, "The Holy Spirit will do a miracle in you so that the One born to you will be the Holy One, the Son of God."

The Coming of Jesus Part Two

"I am the Lord's servant" Mary said, "Let His will be done just as you have said". Then the angel left her, and the baby began growing inside of Mary.

When Mary was almost ready to have her baby, she and Joseph had to go to Bethlehem, Joseph's hometown, to pay a special tax. When they arrived there, it was time for the baby to be born, but there was no room available for them anyplace. All they could find was a stable for animals. When Jesus was born, Mary and Joseph wrapped him with cloths and laid Him in a manger. A manger was a feeding trough filled with hay and livestock feed. Curious animals stood around it.

In the fields nearby that night, there were some shepherds who were watching their sheep. They were afraid when they saw a bright light shine all around them and an angel coming down to speak to them. "Do not be afraid, I have come to bring you good news that will give great joy to everyone. Today in Bethlehem, the town of David, a Savior has been born to you. He is Christ the Lord. You will find Him wrapped in cloths and lying in a manger."

Just then the sky was filled with angels praising God and shouting, "Glory to God in the highest and peace to all mankind to whom God is sending His greatest gift." Then these shepherds hurried off and found Mary and Joseph and the baby lying in a manger just as the angels had told them. When they had seen the baby, they told everyone they could what they had seen and what the angels had told them.

What Jesus Did Here on Earth

When Jesus grew up, He did many miracles, like healing the sick and crippled and quieting terrible storms and even raising the dead. He was showing the people that He was the One the prophets wrote about. The devil was very concerned and got his followers, called demons, to torment people. But Jesus was stronger than Satan and cast the demons out of the people.

Many of the leaders of the country hated Jesus because He did such things as healing people on the Sabbath, which is like our Sunday today. But Jesus told them that God made every day for doing good! So they secretly made plans to arrest Him and have Him crucified. But Jesus knew that what they meant for harm would free men, women, boys, and girls from their sins.

Satan and his demons knew why Jesus had come to earth. When Adam and Eve disobeyed God and sinned, it gave Satan and the devils who followed him power over mankind. Jesus came to break that power and rescue those who trusted in Him. He would remove them from Satan's world and bring them into the kingdom of God.

Jesus taught us how to live for God by his preaching and how He lived here on earth. And by His death on a cross, He would pay for our sins. This was the reason He came. That and to defeat the devil and destroy the evil things he does.

Many followed Jesus, but there were 12 special men that He called to follow Him. They were called disciples and taught others how to follow Jesus and be children of God.

The Death of Jesus

These disciples followed Jesus everywhere while learning from Him how to carry on His work after He died. Jesus told them not to be sad because three days after He died, He would rise from the dead and go back to the Father and send the Holy Spirit to be with them and help them.

Before He was arrested, Jesus led His disciples to a garden called Gethsemane. He knew He would soon suffer and die for our sins, and He sweat drops of blood as He knelt to pray.

He prayed, "Father, I have taught the people how to live for You in a fallen and evil world. I have taught My disciples how to carry on My work, and it is now time for Me to finish the work You sent Me to do. You will give eternal life to all those people who love Me and believe in Me because you love Me and love them. You have given them to be Mine and be with Me forever.

"I am coming to You Father, back to the glory I had with you before the world was made, which I left behind to become a man and die for the world's sins. I pray, Father, that You will love those who believe in Me just as you love Me, and You will protect them from Satan and his devils." Jesus was now ready to face the cross.

Then the soldiers came carrying torches and lanterns and swords. Jesus knew what was happening and went out and let them arrest Him and asked them to let His disciples go. They brought Jesus to court and sentenced Him to be crucified. It was there that God put all our sins on Him and had Him die for us, even though He never did even one thing wrong.

Jesus Rises from the Dead

They took Jesus down from the cross and put Him in a tomb. It was late and they had to hurry. His followers would come back later and finish the burial. But something wonderful happened. When two women came to finish His burial, two angels were sitting where His body had been. The angels said to them, "Why are you looking for people who are alive where dead people are? He is not here He has risen from the dead!"

As they ran off to tell the other disciples of what they had seen and heard, they met Jesus. They knelt down and worshipped Him, and He told them, "Don't be afraid."

Later, he told His disciples, "I have defeated death for you and opened a way to heaven for everyone who loves Me and believes in Me. Now I am going back to My Father and Your Father.

"I want you to tell others about Me so they will believe as you believe and follow Me here on earth and in heaven to come. I want you to love Me and follow Me and live for Me. I will come back once again and set up my perfect kingdom here on earth. Then there will be no more death or pain or sorrow.

"In the meantime, I will reward everyone who serves Me. Always remember that I love you and will always be with you through the power of the Holy Spirit. For He will live in you and help you live for Me."

www.ingramcontent.com/pod-product-compliance
Lightning Source LLC
Chambersburg PA
CBHW061148010526
44118CB00026B/2909